doggie
dinners

by Joe Inglis

Public Eye Publications

A Public Eye Publications Book

www.thegreatestintheworld.com

Design and layout: The DesignCouch
www.designcouch.co.uk

Editor: Steve Brookes

Copy editor: Bronwyn Robertson
www.theartsva.com

This first edition published in 2007 by
Public Eye Publications, PO Box 3182,
Stratford-upon-Avon, Warwickshire CV37 7XW

All enquiries regarding any extracts or re-use of any material
in this book should be addressed to the publishers.
A CIP catalogue record for this book is available from the British Library
ISBN 9781-905151-15-8

Printed and bound by Biddles Books Limited, King's Lynn, Norfolk PE30 4LS

dedicated to Jack

*The best spotty black
and white dog in the world!*

introduction

Man and dogs have been the best of friends for many thousands of years – in fact there is evidence that we were sharing our meals with canine companions as long as 12,000 years ago. And during this time, we've become more and more involved in what our dogs are eating – from throwing them a leftover bone from the fireside, right up to the modern complete diet.

My personal interest in canine nutrition started at vet school, more than ten years ago, and ever since I've been fascinated by the effect diet can have on the health and happiness of pet dogs. Unfortunately, many cheap commercial dog foods are full of the very worst ingredients you could imagine, including all sorts of chemicals and additives – and it's easy to spot the dogs that live on these kinds of diets, with their dull coats, weak immune systems and generally poor health. But over the last decade there has been a shift away from these diets, in favour of more natural, healthy dog foods, which are made with the kind of ingredients you or I would find acceptable – and the results have been great to see, with more and more dogs enjoying better health as a result.

But – and it's a big but – dried food, no matter how good it is, can get a little dull and repetitive after a while; imagine if you were asked to live on nothing but one type of food for the rest of your life! So, when I took on Jack as a puppy, I started to think about whether I could cook him the occasional fresh meal at home to add a little variety and interest to his diet. Months of kitchen research and experimentation followed, as I created recipes that I knew from my veterinary knowledge would be safe and healthy for him – and that he approved of by wolfing down!

The end result has been far more successful than I ever imagined when I first mixed together some chicken mince and rice in Jack's bowl. He loves his weekly fresh meals – and I've loved the process of creating them; and I'm really excited at the prospect of dogs all over the world sharing Jack's enjoyment – and reaping the health benefits as well.

All of the recipes are designed to be occasional meals, rather than a replacement for your dog's regular healthy dried food. There are once-a-week meals for a regular dose of fresh food, as well as one-offs for those special occasions such as birthdays, and even recipes you can happily share with your dog.

So have a read through, try a few recipes out, and you'll soon have one happy, healthy dog on your hands!

Enjoy!

Joe Inglis

contents

Before you start…

There are a few things to go through before we get stuck into the cooking, just to help you understand the theory behind these recipes – and to give you guidelines, should you want to experiment!

Firstly, and most importantly, you have to always remember that you are cooking for a dog and not for a person. Dogs and people have different nutritional needs and some foods that are fine for people can be dangerous to dogs – and vice versa. And don't forget that some flavours which you might find horrible will be the ones that your dog absolutely loves, so be prepared to hold your nose and work through the smell barrier for your dog!

Secondly, some of the recipes use an ingredient called brewer's yeast which you might not be aware of. It's basically the pasteurised residue of commercial brewed beer and it's packed full of all sorts of nutrients including protein and vitamins. You can buy it in powder or tablet form from your local health store, and it's well worth getting a jar if you're keen on following a few of these recipes.

And finally, some tips on what you can and can't use in recipes for dogs. The most important foods to avoid are:

 Tomatoes – a small amount of ripe tomato is unlikely to cause any problems, but green tomatoes can cause serious stomach upsets and even heart problems, so it's best to avoid them.

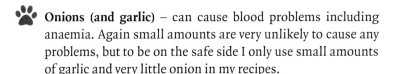 **Onions (and garlic)** – can cause blood problems including anaemia. Again small amounts are very unlikely to cause any problems, but to be on the safe side I only use small amounts of garlic and very little onion in my recipes.

Grapes and raisins – both can cause very serious illness including kidney problems, and large amounts have been known to be fatal to dogs, so avoid wherever possible.

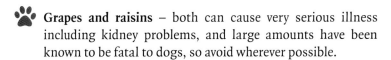 **Chocolate** – one of the ingredients of chocolate, theobromine, is related to caffeine, and some dogs react very badly to it, showing signs such as hyper-excitability, increased heart rate and muscle tremors. Dark chocolates contain the highest levels of theobromine, but I'd advise keeping all chocolate away from dogs.

Mushrooms – best avoided as some dogs will not tolerate mushrooms well and they can cause serious toxicity.

On the other side of the equation, there are a few rather surprising ingredients that are really healthy for your dog, such as:

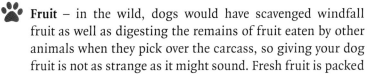 **Fruit** – in the wild, dogs would have scavenged windfall fruit as well as digesting the remains of fruit eaten by other animals when they pick over the carcass, so giving your dog fruit is not as strange as it might sound. Fresh fruit is packed

full of antioxidants, vitamins and all sorts of other healthy nutrients, so it's great for keeping your dog in top condition. The only tricky part is persuading him that he really does want to eat fruit – which is where some of my more ingenious recipes involving fruit and liver come in!

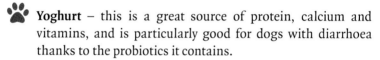 **Yoghurt** – this is a great source of protein, calcium and vitamins, and is particularly good for dogs with diarrhoea thanks to the probiotics it contains.

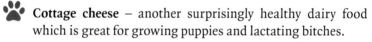 **Cottage cheese** – another surprisingly healthy dairy food which is great for growing puppies and lactating bitches.

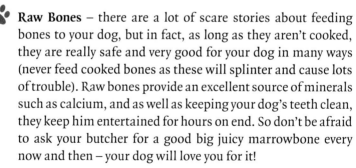 **Raw Bones** – there are a lot of scare stories about feeding bones to your dog, but in fact, as long as they aren't cooked, they are really safe and very good for your dog in many ways (never feed cooked bones as these will splinter and cause lots of trouble). Raw bones provide an excellent source of minerals such as calcium, and as well as keeping your dog's teeth clean, they keep him entertained for hours on end. So don't be afraid to ask your butcher for a good big juicy marrowbone every now and then – your dog will love you for it!

everyday meals

Variety is the spice of life, and these everyday recipes
are an ideal way to liven up your dog's dinner once
a week or so. If you find yourself with a bit of spare time
one evening, or just fancy treating the dog to something
special as a reward for not digging up the rose garden,
cook up one of these doggy delights and he'll be your
best friend for the rest of the day!

 # chicken & rice

Let's start with something really easy – and very healthy. This dish was the inspiration behind Joe & Jack's Fresh Chicken and Rice complete food, and it combines one of the healthiest proteins available – chicken – with rice which is an easily digestible carbohydrate, and a mixture of veg which provide lots of vitamins and minerals. It's great for all dogs, including those with sensitive digestions and older dogs.

It's ideal for freezing, so you can store it in single-serving sized bags, then simply defrost a tasty and healthy meal the next time you want to give your dog something special.

YOU'LL NEED (for a couple of medium dog portions)

- 225g chicken mince
- 200g rice (preferably brown)
- 1 small carrot, finely grated
- 150g fresh peas
- 1 teaspoon Marmite

1 Boil the rice in a large pan of boiling water. When the rice is almost cooked (1–2 minutes away), drop the grated carrot and peas into the water and let it simmer until the rice is done. This makes the veg much more digestible, without losing all of its goodness. When the rice is cooked, drain well.

2 Meanwhile, fry the mince for a few minutes until it is browned – you shouldn't need to add any oil as there is plenty of fat in the mince – and add it to the rice.

3 Finally, mix in the yeast extract and serve once cooled. Prepare yourself for a slobbery lick of gratitude!

Did you know ...
that raw eggs can cause a dietary deficiency and lead to skin disease?

everyday meals

🐾 meatballs & marrowbone gravy

This is a great recipe which smells as good as it tastes – Jack knows this is on the menu as soon as the oven door opens – even if he's at the other end of the garden! It's a good all round recipe, suitable for most dogs, although not ideal for elderly pooches, due to the rich nature of the beef mince.

YOU'LL NEED (for the meatballs)

- 225g lean beef mince
- 50g cheddar cheese, grated
- 1 small carrot, grated
- ½ cup of breadcrumbs
- 1 egg
- 1 small clove of garlic, crushed
- 1 teaspoon of brewer's yeast

1 You don't need a degree in home economics to make these meatballs – just mix everything together in a big bowl and then scoop it out and shape it into balls. Pop them onto a greased baking tray and cook them for about 30 minutes (until they're oozing cheese!) in a moderate oven (180°C/ 350°F/Gas 4). This will make enough for several meals. For a good meal, feed one meatball for every 5 kg your dog weighs, and freeze the rest for next time.

YOU'LL NEED (for the marrowbone gravy)

- 1 large meaty marrow bone cut into pieces from your friendly butcher
- 25g plain flour
- 25g butter

2 Cover the bone with water and bring to the boil. Then let it simmer for about an hour – during which time your dog will be your constant companion as the house fills with the lovely meaty aromas!

3 When you can stand the constant begging no more, banish the dog to the garden and set about making the gravy, by cooking the flour in the fat until it forms a rich brown paste (about 5 minutes). Then add half a pint of the stock from the bones – along with any meaty chunks and marrow you can scrape off the bones – and mix it all together over a medium heat for a couple of minutes.

4 When the meatballs and gravy are suitably cooled, pour the gravy over the meatballs. Then release the dog in from the garden, stand back and watch him wolf it down!

everyday meals

 fishy delight

Fish is a great source of healthy protein for your dog, and it also contains high levels of omega-3 oils which are great for the heart. On the downside, raw fish can interfere with the uptake of some vitamins, so it's best avoided.

This simple recipe makes enough for several servings and it has an extra boost of calcium from the ground eggshells, which makes it ideal for young growing dogs and whelping bitches, as well as being a good everyday dish.

YOU'LL NEED

- 500g boneless white fish
- 1 small tin oily fish (sardines or pilchards)
- 1 cup rice (brown if possible)
- 3 eggs
- 1 carrot, grated

1 Steam the fish (or boil if you prefer) for about 20 minutes – until it is flaky and cooked through. At the same time, cook the rice according to the instructions on the packet, and hardboil the eggs. Put the grated carrot into the rice water a couple of minutes before it's cooked, just to make it more digestible.

2 Once the fish, rice and carrot are cooked, mix them all together in a large bowl. Take the shell off the eggs – but don't throw it away – and break up the eggs into small chunks, then mix them into the fish and rice mixture. Scoop up the shell and grind it into as fine a powder as you can with a pestle and mortar (or rolling pin if it's all you've got), adding about a teaspoon into the mix. The grittiness of the calcium in the shell helps clean your dog's teeth as he eats.

3 Finally, pour in the tinned fish complete with all the oil and mix everything together thoroughly. Sprinkle a little parsley over the top if you fancy – but don't expect the dog to take any notice – it'll get wolfed down with the rest of it!

Did you know ...

that tinned dog foods are about 80% water? That might sound a lot, but it's about the same as fresh meat!

everyday meals

 # kidney casserole

There are few things better for your dog to eat every now and then than a bit of kidney. It's packed full of good quality protein, essential fatty acids and loads of vitamins. The only downside is it tastes a bit of wee – but dogs don't seem to mind one little bit!

YOU'LL NEED (to make a jumbo dish of casserole)

- 125g stewing steak, diced
- 2 lambs' kidneys, chopped into quarters
- 20g plain flour
- 1 teaspoon Marmite
- 1 tablespoon oil
- 1 small swede, diced (approx 250g)
- 1 small carrot, diced

1 Roll the kidneys and diced steak in the flour. Then heat the oil in a large saucepan and stir in the Marmite. Drop the floury meat into the oil, and cook for a few minutes until it's all nice and brown. Then add the diced veg and cook for another couple of minutes.

2 Finally, add enough water to cover all the ingredients, put the lid on, turn the heat down, and leave to simmer for about an hour.

3 When the dog's patience is finally exhausted and he can wait no more, spoon out the bone and discard it (somewhere where the dog can't get to it!), and let the stew cool down before pouring a generous ladle-full on top of a handful of his normal dried biscuits and serving with a smile!

NUTRITION TIP

Dogs are great at wolfing down dried dog biscuits because they produce lots of saliva in their mouths to help lubricate the food on its way down. They evolved this ability because eating quickly is very useful in the wild when there are lots of other animals after you and your lunch!

everyday meals

pasta with chicken & veg

Apparently pasta has been eaten by us humans for over 5,000 years – so it's about time we started sharing some of this healthy carbohydrate with our best friends! Pasta is healthy because it's low in fat and salt, and rich in highly digestible carbohydrate which is essential for making energy.

This recipe combines pasta with healthy protein from chicken and a few puréed veg, to make a meal which is suitable for all dogs – and especially those active hounds who spend all their time chasing balls in the park.

YOU'LL NEED (to fuel one medium-sized dog)

- 50g pasta – any shape will do
- 1 chicken drumstick
- 100g assorted veg (anything will do!)
- 1 teaspoon brewer's yeast (optional)

1   This is a really easy one – just boil a large pan of water, drop the drumsticks in and simmer for ten minutes. Then add the pasta and cook for another 10–12 minutes until it is nice and soft. Cooking the pasta with the chicken means it'll taste meaty, making it much more appetising to dogs.

3 While the pasta and chicken are simmering away, take any odd bits of leftover raw veg you can find – carrots, broccoli, beans – anything will do except tomatoes, mushrooms and onions – and chuck them into a food processor. Blend them together until they form a rich purée, and leave it in the processor for now.

4 Drain the pasta and chicken when the pasta is still quite firm (or al denté as they say in Italy). This will give the dish a bit more texture, which is important for palatability. Take out the chicken and remove the bones. Then add the chicken meat to the veg in the blender and whiz it up until it is all finely chopped together, adding in the brewer's yeast if you have some. Then mix the chicken and veg paste in with the pasta, cool and serve.

NUTRITION TIP

Feed a young puppy (8–12 weeks old) at least three times a day and four times when they are just weaned. You can drop this down to two meals a day once they are three months old.

everyday meals

 liver dumplings

The liver is the engine of the body, so it's no surprise that it's full of all sorts of vital nutrients. It's packed full of vitamins, including vitamin A which is vital for eyesight, and is also a good source of minerals including iron. Too much raw liver can cause problems, but feeding this cooked liver recipe once a week is fine.

The recipe makes about 8 dumplings, which are best fed mixed in with some dried food.

YOU'LL NEED (to fuel one medium-sized dog)

- 200g beef or chicken liver, diced finely or blended
- 100g breadcrumbs
- 50ml hot water
- 1 egg, beaten
- 2 stock cubes or 1 meaty marrowbone

1 Soften the breadcrumbs with enough hot water to make them sticky, and then mix in the diced or blended liver and beaten egg. Leave this to stand for half an hour so that it becomes firm – why not walk the dog to get his appetite up?

2 When you get back, moisten your hands and then shape the mixture into small round dumplings. Drop these into a large pan of boiling stock made by dissolving a couple of stock cubes in a litre and a half of water. Alternatively, if you've got a raw marrowbone from the butcher, boil that up in the water instead for a really meaty taste.

3 Cook the dumplings uncovered for 15 minutes and then fish them out and serve once cooled. If you're feeling really keen, you can also freeze the stock you have left behind (complete with any bits of failed dumpling that might well be floating about!). Put it in an ice-cube tray and thaw out one cube every now and then to spice up his dinner with a nice bit of liver gravy.

Did you know …

that dogs can catch worms from eating fleas?

meaty parsnip mash

This is one of Jack's all time favourites – and I must admit to being rather partial to a spoonful myself. It's full of real meaty chunks, which dogs love, as well as plenty of veg for vitamins, and cheese for calcium. Not one for the older dog as there's too much rich protein, but ideal for all other dogs.

YOU'LL NEED

- 250g stewing steak, diced *
- 1 teaspoon oil
- A couple of medium potatoes (around 350g)
- A couple of parsnips (around 200g)
- 1 carrot
- ½ teaspoon Marmite
- 100g cheddar cheese, grated

I like to use the toughest steak I can find for this recipe. Dogs love chewing their food, and it helps keep their teeth clean as well. Just watch your own teeth if you try a bit!

1. The first step is to get a big pan of water on to boil while you chop up all the veg. Wash them to get rid of any nasty chemicals, but don't peel them as this removes a lot of the goodness. Put all of the veg in together and let it simmer for about 15 minutes – until it's all quite soft.

2. Meanwhile, fry up the diced steak in the oil. Don't worry about cooking it all the way through – dogs love rare meat.

3. When the veg is done, drain off the water and set about it with a masher until you've got a thick mash in the pan. Then mix in the Marmite, cheese and fried steak. Mix it all together and then let it cool. Serve on its own or mixed in with some dried biscuits.

NUTRITION TIP

If your dog is a fussy eater, it pays to be strong and not give in – it won't hurt him not to eat for a day or even longer, so you can win the battle of wills, as most dogs will give in eventually when they're hungry enough!

everyday meals

home-cooked turkey kibbles

There's nothing better for your dog's teeth than crunching on hard foods such as dried kibbles. But feeding the same old biscuits day after day can get a little dull for the dog, so here's a recipe for some healthy home-cooked kibbles that can be mixed in with his normal dinner, or fed as an alternative every now and then.

YOU'LL NEED

- 225g turkey mince
- 100g rice (brown is healthier than white)
- 1 dessertspoon oil
- 1 clove garlic
- 1 small carrot
- 1 egg
- 1 teaspoon brewer's yeast (optional)

1 Boil the rice according to the instructions on the packet, and when it's cooked, drain off the water and leave it to stand.

2 Meanwhile, fry up the crushed garlic for a few minutes before adding the mince and cooking over a gentle heat for 7–10 minutes. While this is cooking, purée the carrot in a blender (or grate finely if you don't have a blender), and add it to the rice.

3 Beat the egg into the mixture, but don't throw away the shell. Instead, drop it into a small pan of boiling water and simmer for five minutes. This will kill off any nasty bugs like salmonella. Drain the water and then grind the shell up in a pestle and mortar or under a rolling pin until it's a fine powder. Add about a teaspoon of the powder to the rice mixture. This adds calcium to the kibbles, balancing the relatively low-calcium mince and rice.

4 Next, mix the mince (and brewer's yeast if you have some) into the rice mixture and blend it all together to form a thick paste (if you don't have a blender you can just mix it thoroughly by hand, but it is harder to form good kibbles this way). While it's cooling down, put the oven on to warm up (200°C/400F/Gas 6). Then grease a baking tray or two, and form the mixture into cherry-sized balls. Place these on the baking trays and put them in the oven for 45 minutes, until they are hard and crunchy.

🐾 trout & oat cakes with a fishy gravy

Oats are one of the healthiest sources of carbohydrate for your dog – they contain lots of minerals including calcium, which is vital for healthy bones, as well as being rich in soluble fibre. This recipe, which combines the goodness of oats with the healthy fish oils found in trout, is perfect for all dogs, little and large, and can be fed as often as you like.

YOU'LL NEED

- 1 medium sized fresh trout
- 2 medium potatoes (about 300g)
- 50g butter
- 1 tablespoon parsley, chopped
- 1 egg yolk
- 2 tablespoons plain flour
- 1 egg
- 50g rolled oats
- 1 tablespoon oil

1 Boil the spuds (skins on, cut into chunks) until they are soft, and then mash them with half of the butter.

2 Meanwhile, separately boil the whole trout in a pan of water for ten minutes. Then fish it out, without losing the water, and remove the flesh from the bones. Put the bones, head and skin back into the water and let it simmer for half an hour.

3 Add the de-boned fish, parsley, half the butter and the egg yolk to the mashed potato and mix thoroughly. Form the mixture into about 6 fish cakes and leave them in the fridge to chill for about an hour.

4 While the cakes are chilling, gently cook 2 tablespoons of the flour with the remaining butter for a minute or so, and then gradually add ½ pint of the stock from the simmering fish remains. Continue to stir until the gravy thickens, before turning off the heat and leaving to cool.

5 Remove the cakes from the fridge and dust them in flour. Then beat the egg and dip each cake into it, before rolling them in the oat flakes. Then fry the cakes for 5 minutes on each side in the oil.

6 Once the cakes have cooled, pour over the gravy and serve.

Did you know that big dogs can suffer from twisted stomachs if they eat too much and run around too soon after a meal? Make sure you let your dog digest his dinner before a big walk!

# joe & jack's stew

This is an easy recipe which uses Joe & Jack's biscuits, so it makes a healthy and tasty everyday dish. The added meat and veg complement the kibbles really well, and add fresh nutrients as well as extra taste.

YOU'LL NEED (to make enough for several helpings)

- 200g Joe & Jack's biscuits
- 750ml water
- 250g stewing steak
- 1 carrot
- 1 potato

1 Put the kibble and water into a large saucepan and bring to the boil. Then let it simmer for about twenty minutes. After about ten minutes, start to mash up the softened kibbles with a wooden spoon, and keep going at it until you've formed a thick and smooth gravy. Add more water if the mixture is getting too thick.

2 Meanwhile, dice the steak and veg, and cook them in a large pan of boiling water for twenty minutes. When the veg is soft and the meat cooked through, drain off the water, and mix into the kibble gravy.

everyday meals

lamb stew with croutons

There's nothing quite like this hearty stew for warming the inner dog after he's been out for a long winter walk. It's full of healthy veg and low in fat and salt, which makes it another great all-rounder. Best served warm, on a cold day.

YOU'LL NEED (to make enough for a pack of hungry hounds)

- 250g lamb or mutton, diced
- 1 carrot
- 1 potato
- 1 apple
- 1 cup stale bread

1 This is one of the easiest recipes around. Simply cover the lamb with cold water in a large pan, bring to the boil and simmer for 1 hour. While this is bubbling away, chop up the carrots, potatoes and apples into rough chunks, and break up the bread into small pieces. Cook the bread in a low oven for half an hour, so that it is crisp but not burnt.

2 Add the carrot, potato and apple to the lamb after an hour, and simmer it all together for about 7–8 minutes – until the veg are partially cooked but still firm. Then allow to cool, but serve while it is still warm. Mix in the bread croutons at the last minute so they stay crunchy.

treats

A relationship with a dog is a two way thing – you throw a stick, he brings it back; you clean the house, he covers it in mud and hair – that kind of thing. And there are times when only a treat will do as your way of rewarding him for good behaviour. So when he next behaves himself at the vet, or doesn't attack the next door neighbour's cat, cook up one of these recipes and treat him to something special to say 'well done'.

All of these recipes are designed to be both super-tasty and healthy as well, so as long as you are sensible with your rewards, you don't have to worry that your treats are contributing to his waistline.

liver & bacon chews

In my mind there are few smells as appealing as that of bacon gently crisping in a pan. And it's not just me that thinks like this – Jack, and every dog I've ever known, also loves bacon, which is why these lovely chewy treats are such a winner.

They're made of crunchy pieces of bacon in a chewy dough made from liver, egg and flour, and they are brilliant as training bribes (Jack learnt how to shake hands in one afternoon with a tray of these treats!).

So cook up a batch and keep them to hand for an occasional reward or training titbit.

YOU'LL NEED (to make several helpings)

- 225g liver
- 1 egg
- 1 cup plain flour
- ¼ teaspoon oregano
- 2 rashers bacon

1 Fry the bacon until just crisp, and then allow it to cool before cutting up into tiny pieces. Keep the fat from the cooking as you'll need that in a minute.

2 Next, put the liver into the blender and whiz until it forms a thick red sludge. Pour in the fat from the frying pan (wait until it has cooled a little), break in the egg and sprinkle in the oregano. Fire up the blender again and continue to mix for a few seconds, until it forms a nice, uniform paste. Then pour it into a large mixing bowl, add in the bacon and mix well.

3 Finally, mix in the flour to form a thick dough which you can roll out and divide into grape-sized pieces. Place these on a well-greased baking tray and cook in a moderate oven for half an hour.

Did you know ...
that some dogs lack the enzyme lactase which means they can't digest cow's milk and can suffer from diarrhoea if they are fed dairy products?

frozen nutty yoghurt

This is the ideal summertime doggy treat – and health-wise it's pretty good as well. Yoghurt is basically milk that has had the sugar converted to lactic acid by bacteria, and it's these bacteria that give yoghurt its healthy properties. It's full of calcium for strong bones, good quality protein, and vitamins A and B. The peanut butter is high in fat, but dogs do need fat as it contains lots of essential fatty acids as well as providing energy.

This treat is really ideal for working or active dogs who've been out in the hot summer burning off lots of energy.

YOU'LL NEED (to make several helpings)
- 1 large pot of plain live yoghurt
- 4 dessertspoons peanut butter

1 Put the peanut butter into a microwave-safe dish and cook in the microwave until soft (30 seconds). Then mix into the yoghurt in a large bowl and pour into paper cupcake cases. Place these on a tray and freeze them.

2 To serve, simply whip one out of the freezer when you come in, and turn it out into the dog's bowl.

treats

Fat is not all bad – as well
as being an excellent source
of energy for your dog,
it also provides her with
lots of vital vitamins and
essential fatty acids.

great balls of egg!

If you want to have a bit of fun with your dog, these treats are great. They are basically hard balls of oatmeal pastry wrapped around a hardboiled egg, and are designed to keep your dog happy as she chases it around trying to crack it open and get to the tasty egg and cheese centre.

The recipe makes 5, but they need to be eaten within a few days, so why not give away a few to doggie-loving friends (or if you're feeling mean, pass them off as Scotch Eggs at a dinner party!).

YOU'LL NEED (to make 5 balls)

- 50g butter or margarine
- 75g rolled oats
- 75g plain flour
- 6 eggs
- ½ teaspoon Marmite
- 50g cheese, grated

1 Firstly, hardboil 5 of the six eggs (about 8 minutes is fine) and remove the shells.

2 Then to make the crunchy outer, rub the butter, oats and flour together to form a crumbly mix. Beat in the remaining egg, mix in the Marmite and gradually add just enough hot water to make a sticky, but firm, dough. Roll this out thinly on a floury board and cut into five equal squares.

3 Now sprinkle a little cheese on each square, and place an egg in the middle of each one. Wrap up the dough to completely enclose the egg and place the finished balls on a well-greased baking tray. Cook for 25 minutes in a moderate oven, allow to cool and let the games begin!

NUTRITION TIP
Give the dog a bone when he's hungry not when he's just eaten if you don't want him to dig a hole in lawn and bury it!

bacon flapjacks

Flapjacks are one of my personal favourites, and they can also make a good tasty dog treat. They're made mainly of oats, which are one of the best sources of carbohydrate for your dog, as they're high in essential fatty acids, protein and minerals, including the all-important calcium.

Their usual downside is the high levels of sugar and fat, but I've reduced both in this recipe so it's not too rich – however, I'd still be cautious about offering this to your dog if he's having trouble with his weight, and in general it's definitely a recipe to cook, store, and give in small amounts.

YOU'LL NEED (to make 5 balls)

- 100g margarine
- 125g porridge oats
- 50g self-raising flour
- 2 tablespoons cornflour
- 1 teaspoon mustard
- 2 tablespoons olive oil
- 2 rashers bacon

1 Fry the bacon until crispy and, when cool, cut into little pieces. Keep the oil from the pan to hand.

2 Meanwhile, mix together the margarine, oats, flour and cornflour in a large bowl. Add in the mustard, chopped bacon and olive oil, mix thoroughly and then press into a greased baking tray. Drizzle the remaining fat in the frying pan over the mixture before putting it into a hot oven (190°C/375°F/Gas 5) for 20 minutes.

NUTRITION TIP

If your dog has bad skin, it could be an allergy to something in his diet. Your vet will help to make any diagnosis of food allergy or intolerance, but in general avoiding foods with beef, wheat and dairy products is a good idea if you suspect a food problem.

treats

🐾 fruit shake

It might surprise you, but in the wild, dogs would eat quite a lot of fruit. This comes from eating the remains of other animals that have themselves eaten fruit, and from picking up windfalls. It provides a great supply of energy in the form of readily available fruit sugars, as well as all the vitamins and antioxidants we associate with fruit.

So this recipe, which is stuffed full of the goodness of raw fruit, is one of the healthiest in the book and the addition of a bit of yoghurt also adds to its healthy qualities and makes it more palatable. Some dogs will lap this up on its own, but for the average, fast-food loving hound, you might need to pour it over his everyday dinner to get the goodness down him.

YOU'LL NEED (for several portions)

- 1 banana
- 1 apple
- A few strawberries
- 1 orange
- 1 small pot of yoghurt (125ml)

1. Put the peeled banana (watch out where you put the skin...), apple and strawberries into a blender and whiz them up until they are well and truly puréed. Pour into a bowl and add in the peeled and chopped up orange. Finally, mix in the yoghurt and give it a good stir.

2. Try this out but if he turns his nose up, you can try either pouring it over his dried dog kibbles, or adding half a tin of wet meaty dog food to the shake mixture.

Did you know ...

that tit-bits are unhealthy? Your dog might love your leftovers but they tend to be the least healthy bits of your food and are often very fatty.

 meaty jelly

Don't make the dog feel left out the next time you have a children's party – make him his own jelly so he can join in the fun! (Just be careful not to confuse this with the kids' version – they won't thank you if you serve them meaty jelly instead of strawberry!).

This recipe even manages to be quite healthy, as there's none of the sugar you'd get with a normal jelly – just lots of tasty meat juices and chunks of steak!

YOU'LL NEED (to make a pint of jelly)

- 1 small piece of stewing steak (about 150g)
- 1 small carrot
- 1 stock cube
- 1 tablespoon gelatine

1 Chop the steak and carrot into small pieces and drop them into a pan of boiling water (at least 1 litre). Add in the stock cube and simmer for about half an hour, and then remove the carrot and meat from the water and put them to one side.

2 Pour about 10ml or ¼ pint of the broth into a mixing bowl and add in the gelatine, mix thoroughly and then top up to a pint (450ml) with the broth.

3 Allow the mixture to cool before pouring a little into the bottom of a suitable mould (cat-shaped perhaps?). Put the mould into the fridge and wait for it to start to set (this may take an hour or more). Then add in a few small pieces of the meat, and cover with another layer of jelly liquid. Repeat this, allowing the jelly to set as you go, until you have filled the mould(s) and used up all the meat.

4 Put back in the fridge to set completely and serve with some Frozen Nutty Yoghurt.

Did you know ...
that dogs can eat cat food safely, but cats shouldn't eat dog food?

stink bombs

Not the most endearing name perhaps, but it kind of stuck when my wife Jenny first smelt this recipe being cooked in the kitchen!

These easy to cook treats are made with strong parmesan cheese that will appeal to most dogs, and also contain healthy turkey mince and sweet potato and oats for carbohydrate.

YOU'LL NEED (for several portions)

- 225g turkey mince
- ½ cup parmesan cheese, grated
- 1 small sweet potato
- 1 cup quick oats

1   Boil the sweet potato, and mash when done. Then mix all the ingredients together in a bowl and form into walnut-sized balls. Bake these in a moderate oven for about 20 minutes and voilá – your house will smell of cheese, but the dog will have a smile on his face!

2   Store these treats in the fridge for a couple of days or freeze them if you don't use them up.

treats

puppy food

Healthy nutrition is one of the most important things to get right when you're bringing up a puppy, which is why I would recommend that you generally stick to a proper complete diet at this time. Getting the right mix of essential protein, vitamins and minerals is hard to achieve with home cooked recipes if that is all you are feeding, whereas the complete diets have been specially formulated to contain everything a growing puppy needs.

However, that's not to say there isn't a place for the occasional puppy treat and special meal. Try out these recipes alongside your puppy's complete diet, and they'll give her an extra dose of healthy fresh nutrients – as well as making her love you even more!

 # puppy breakfast

There's not a puppy in the world who wouldn't love this dish. It's not something I'd give every morning, but as a weekly treat it's a great way of boosting their intake of calcium and protein. So if you're making yourself a fry up on a Sunday morning, why not spare an egg and a bit of bacon for the puppy – you never know, she might reward you with a lie-in next week…

YOU'LL NEED (to make one small dish)

- 1 egg
- 1 rasher bacon
- 1 tablespoon cottage cheese*

* *It's best to avoid the low fat cottage cheese as this tends to contain too much salt for puppies.*

1 To make the meal, just hardboil the egg (for about 8–9 minutes), and then remove the shell and mash the egg together with the cottage cheese. Grind the shell up with a pestle and mortar or rolling pin and add ½ teaspoon of the powder into the mix. This adds calcium and texture to the meal.

2 Then grill the bacon lightly, and chop it up into small pieces. Mix it into the egg and cheese, and serve once cooled.

meaty rice pudding

Something of a treat, this recipe is packed full of wholesome nutrients – carbohydrate from the rice, protein from the meat and calcium from the milk. It takes a while to cook, and the recipe makes enough for several meals – but you can keep it in the fridge for a few days – or better still, invite around a few friends with puppies and have a puppy party!

YOU'LL NEED (to make enough for a puppy party)

- 125g rice
- 750ml milk
- 150g beef or lamb mince
- 1 teaspoon Marmite

Simply mix all the ingredients together in a large ovenproof dish. Pop it in a moderate oven (180°C/350°F/Gas 4) for about 75 minutes. Stir frequently for the first 45 minutes and then leave alone for the final 30 minutes. Leave it to cool for at least an hour before serving.

puppy cheesy treats

These tasty biscuits are an ideal treat or snack for a hungry puppy. Use them to help with training by rewarding good behaviour – but make sure you don't overdo them as they are quite rich and fatty. One or two treats a day as part of your training schedule is ideal.

YOU'LL NEED (to make enough to last a couple of weeks)

- 250g whole wheat flour
- 150g grated cheddar cheese
- 50g butter
- 1 clove garlic
- 1 beef stock cube
- Milk

1. Mix the flour and butter together in a large bowl and run the fat in until it forms a crumbly mixture. Then add in the grated cheese, crushed garlic and crumbled stock cube and mix well.

2. Slowly add milk to the mixture until it forms a very sticky dough. Flour your hands and start kneading the dough until it forms a single firm lump. Turn it out onto a floured surface and roll it out to about ½ inch thick. Cut the dough up into puppy-sized biscuits using a small pastry cutter – or if you don't have one, try using the end of an apple corer – this cuts the dough into just the right sized little rounds.

3 Then place the biscuits onto a greased baking tray and cook in a moderate oven (180°C/350°F/Gas 4) for 15–20 minutes, until they are golden brown. Allow to cool and then store in an airtight container.

NUTRITION TIP

Weaning puppies onto solid food starts when they are about 3–4 weeks old, and they should be eating just solids by the time they are 8 weeks old. 4 meals a day is ideal for young puppies until they are at least 10 weeks old.

puppy food

🐾 beefy bone

This is a great recipe for really special occasions – perhaps your puppy has just had his vaccinations or passed out of puppy training school. Whatever the occasion, he'll love you for baking these crispy bones which are full of meaty goodness.

YOU'LL NEED (for 4 small bones)

- 50g butter or margarine
- 75g rolled oats
- 75g plain flour
- 1 egg
- ½ teaspoon Marmite
- 2 small leeks
- 125g beef mince

1. Rub the butter, oats and flour together to form a crumbly mix. Then beat in the egg, mix in the Marmite and gradually add just enough hot water to make a sticky but firm dough. Roll this out thinly on a floured board and cut it into 4 rectangles.

2. Next, take both leeks and remove the outer layers until they are about ½ inch thick all the way along. Coat them with a good layer of butter, and then roll two squares of the pastry around each one, leaving a gap in between. You should now have two leeks, each with two sections wrapped in pastry.

3 Lay these on a greased baking sheet, and cook them in a moderate oven for 25 minutes. Then take them out and carefully cut the leeks in half, in between the two sections that are wrapped in pastry. You should then be able to slide the leeks out from the pastry, leaving four firm tubes. Put these back in the oven to cook for a further ten minutes before letting them cool.

4 While the pastry is cooking, fry the mince until cooked through. Then stuff the pastry 'bones' with the meat and voilá, you have four delicious and healthy bones that your puppy will love!

Did you know ...

that an average 20 kilo dog needs about 1000 kcal of energy every day?

liver & banana milkshake

Now this might sound pretty unpleasant to you, but puppies will go mad for this shake. It's full of the goodness of liver, and the fresh vitamins you can only get from fruit such as banana.

Either serve on its own or pour over his dried dog food – either way he'll lap it up.

YOU'LL NEED (for 2 or 3 puppy drinks)

- Small piece of liver (about 100g)
- 1 banana
- 275ml milk

Place the liver in a large bowl and cover it with boiling water. Leave it to cook for ten minutes and then drop it into a blender with the peeled banana and milk. Blend everything together (remember to put the lid on the blender – a mistake I've made once...) and serve straight away.

meals for
special occasions

We all like to mark a special occasion with some kind of
feast, whether it's a meal down the pub on your birthday,
or a romantic dinner for two on Valentine's Day. But what
about our four-legged friends? Well here are a few ideas
for some meals that will let your best friend know how
much he's loved on those special days.

 pooch pizza

Ideal for a doggy birthday, this tasty pizza is healthy thanks to the layer of spinach which provides iron and vitamins, and the low-fat turkey mince on top. The base is made from your dog's normal dried food, so it's got all the goodness he normally gets every day as well as the extra tasty topping.

YOU'LL NEED (for one medium-sized dog pizza)

- 100g dried dog kibble
- 50g plain flour
- 30g butter or margarine
- 100g spinach, finely chopped
- 100g turkey mince
- 50g cheddar cheese, grated

1 Firstly you need to grind up the dried biscuits into a fine powder using a blender. Then moisten the kibble powder with enough warm water to make it into a really moist and gooey mess. Leave it to stand for ten minutes, and add more water if you need to, as the kibble absorbs a lot of water.

2 Next, add in the flour and slightly melted butter, and mix it all together to form a thick dough. It should firm up into a nice dry ball which you can roll out on a floured surface until it's about ¼ inch thick.

3 For the topping, you need to fry up the turkey mince for five minutes or so and then mix it together with the finely chopped spinach. Cover the base with this mixture and finally, sprinkle on the grated cheese.

4 Cook in a moderate oven for 20–25 minutes – until the top is golden brown. Allow to cool thoroughly and then slice into wedges before serving.

Did you know ...

that you can help your dog flight the flab by cutting down their food and adding grated veg their dinner bowl? This will make him feel fuller without adding extra calories.

special occasions

valentine's heart

If the romantic day should come around and there's no-one to share it with this year, why not treat the dog to something truly special? It'll certainly bring you love – but perhaps not quite the kind of love you were looking for! Still, a slobbery kiss from the dog is better than nothing!

YOU'LL NEED (to make your dog's Valentine dreams come true)

- One lamb's heart
- 1 carrot
- 1 leek
- 100g rice

1. Take the heart and cover it with boiling water in a medium sized saucepan (if you want to imagine this as the heart of a jilted lover, feel free!). Add in the chopped carrot and leek and let it all simmer for 15 minutes.

2. In the meantime, cook the rice according to the instructions on the packet and allow it to cool down.

3. When the heart has finished cooking, drain off the water, and carefully slice it into thin strips. Put the cooked carrot and leek into a blender and reduce them to a thick puree.

4 Once everything has cooled down, serve the heart on a bed of rice and top with a spoonful of the vegetable puree. It might not quite be the romantic Valentine's meal you were hoping for, but the dog will love you for making the effort – and you never know, next year might be better!

NUTRITION TIP

Whenever you change your dog's diet, do it gradually over a few days to avoid stomach upsets. Mix in a small amount of the new food with the old on day one, and then gradually increase the amount over 3–4 days until they are settled on the new food.

special occasions

🐾 turkey & trimmings Christmas balls

This is a really quick and easy recipe for a cracking Christmas dinner for your dog. It is really tasty but also a much healthier option than feeding scraps from your Christmas dinner table. It only takes about 20 minutes to prepare and about half an hour in the oven, alongside your turkey.

All the dogs at my surgery (well and ill!) loved this recipe – and the best thing is you'll have most of the ingredients in the fridge ready for your big meal anyway, so it's no real effort to make.

YOU'LL NEED

- 250g turkey mince
- A couple of medium potatoes (around 350g)
- 1 good sized carrot (around 200g)
- A handful of sprouts (about 250g)
- ½ teaspoon of Marmite
- 1 teaspoon cranberry sauce
- Gravy from your Christmas dinner

1 Firstly, boil the potatoes and sprouts for 10–15 minutes until well-cooked. Then drain them and set about them with a masher until they form a rough and sticky mash.

2 Meanwhile, heat up a frying pan and gently brown the mince. You don't need any oil as there is plenty of fat in the meat. Once the mince is cooked through, mix it into the mash, add in the cranberry sauce (great for urinary health), and finally, just to add a healthy dose of B vitamins and a bit of extra meatiness to the flavour, stir in the Marmite (don't worry, dogs aren't like humans – they all love yeast extract!).

3 While the mixture is cooling down, grease a baking tray – and then it's time to get your hands dirty! Form the sticky mix into walnut-sized balls and smooth them off, before placing them on the baking tray.

4 Pop the tray into a moderate oven for half an hour or so – until the balls are nicely crisp and brown – and then take them out and let them stand for at least twenty minutes to cool down. Then arrange them in the dog's bowl, pour over a little gravy and serve.

special occasions

🐾 rabbit casserole with potato dumplings

The ideal way to celebrate Easter and the coming of summer is to cook up this delicious rabbit casserole for the dogs. Rabbit is a healthy, lean meat, and the potato dumplings provide plenty of energy for a long walk or two.

YOU'LL NEED (for the casserole)

- 1 rabbit, chopped up
- A little plain flour
- 1 carrot
- 1 parsnip
- 1 tin vegetable soup

1 Toss the rabbit in the flour and brown it in a saucepan with a little oil. Add in the chopped carrot and parsnip and continue to fry for about 5 minutes. Then pour in the soup and the same quantity of water. Turn down the heat and simmer with the lid on.

2 Meanwhile, you can quickly make the dumplings:

YOU'LL NEED (for the dumplings)

- 250g mashed potato
- A handful of dog kibble (optional)
- 1 egg
- 100g plain flour

3   Simply mix all the ingredients together and form into walnut-sized dumplings. I like to add some kibble into these dumplings because it gives them a bit of texture, but they work fine without.

4   When the casserole has been simmering for half an hour, drop in the dumplings and continue to cook for a further 20 minutes, adding more water if necessary.

5   Let the casserole cool right down and then carefully take out all the rabbit bones. The marrow and flavour from these bones will have been absorbed by the stew and, as eating cooked bones can be dangerous for dogs, make sure none are left in.

This dish freezes well – but don't keep it until next Easter!

birthday cake

What better way to celebrate the dog's big day than with a big, tasty cake? However you can't just bake a normal human cake – it'll be too rich and is likely to upset the dog's digestive tract – and that's the last thing you want on the dog's birthday! So here's a recipe for a healthy doggy birthday cake that won't cause trouble.

YOU'LL NEED (to make a cake big enough for 3 or 4 dogs)

- 250g beef mince
- 1 carrot, grated
- 75g oatmeal
- 75g plain flour
- 30g butter
- 3 eggs
- Yoghurt
- 2 rashers of bacon

1 Fry the mince until brown, add in the grated carrot and continue to cook gently for a few minutes. Meanwhile, mix together the flour and oatmeal and rub in the butter. Beat in the eggs to form a sticky paste, and then add in the mince and carrot, complete with any juice from the pan. Knead the mixture and press it into a well-greased cake tin. Cook for 30 minutes in a moderate oven, turn out and allow to cool.

2 Grill the bacon until crisp and then cut up into small pieces. Cover the cake with yoghurt and sprinkle on the bacon pieces.

summer barbeques

Eating freshly cooked meat straight off the BBQ is one of the great pleasures of the summer – but if you're not careful, it can cause a lot of trouble for dogs. I've seen quite a few dogs in the surgery that have wolfed down BBQ leftovers and have ended up having major surgery to remove a bone from their stomachs. So, not wanting to spend my summer evenings removing bones from dogs, I came up with a few ideas for dog-safe BBQ items. Cook these up especially for the dog, and you'll have a happy hound – and a happy vet!

When working out how much food to feed your dog, trust your eyes and not the feeding guide on the packet.Keep a close eye on your dog's weight, check you can always feel his ribs easily, and you won't go far wrong.

marinated chicken breast

Not quite the marinade you might fancy – but dogs love this recipe! Not one for the older dog, as the Marmite is quite salty.

YOU'LL NEED

- 1 chicken breast
- ½ teaspoon Marmite
- 1 clove garlic

Crush the garlic and mix it into the Marmite. Smear this all over the chicken and let it sit in the fridge for half an hour or so. Then cook it over the BBQ, allow to cool, dice and serve.

Did you know ...

that it's better to feed your dog twice a day than just once? Feed half in the morning and half in the evening – it gives him more to look forward to and is better for his digestion.

steak & kidney burgers

Normal beef burgers are OK for dogs, but if you want to cook up something special that the dog will really love – and which is a lot more healthy for him – try these steak and kidney burgers. The kidney gives extra flavour, as well as essential nutrients such as fatty acids, vitamins and iron. Make up a load and put them in the freezer, so when you have a BBQ, the dog isn't left out!

YOU'LL NEED (makes approximately 10 burgers)

- 250g beef mince
- 250 lamb's kidneys, finely chopped
- 1 small carrot, finely grated
- 2 eggs

---

1 This is another recipe where we're going to use some of the egg shell to add calcium to the recipe. Break the eggs into a bowl and then put the shells on a baking tray and cook them for ten minutes in a moderate oven. This helps to dry them out as well as killing off any nasty bugs. Then grind them up with a pestle and mortar or rolling pin until they form a fine powder.

2 While the egg shells are baking, fry the grated carrot for five minutes in a small amount of oil. Then mix the mince, finely chopped kidney and beaten eggs together, and add in the cooked carrot. Sprinkle ½ teaspoon of the egg shell powder in and knead the mixture together. Then form it into burgers and cook on the BBQ just as you would with a normal burger. Allow to cool and then serve to the dog with some rice or pasta.

NUTRITION TIP

It's important to feed a pregnant bitch more because she needs extra energy for growing the puppies. Add 10% to her rations every week from the 6th week onwards so that she is getting 50% more when she gives birth.

summer barbeques

 # liver & beef kebabs

These are great because there are no bones, and as long as you remember to take the skewer out, they are safe – and dogs love them. All you need for a couple of kebabs is:

YOU'LL NEED

- Diced liver
- Diced stewing steak
- 1 red pepper

Place the liver, steak and pepper alternately on a skewer and BBQ until cooked. Allow to cool thoroughly before sliding off the skewer and into the dog's bowl.

Did you know ...

that you can buy special meat flavoured toothpaste for your dog?

meals to share

Lots of dogs waddle into my surgery after a lifetime
of titbits and leftovers. This kind of diet almost invariably
leads to weight problems, which in turn cause diseases
such as diabetes, heart and liver disease, as well
as making conditions such as arthritis much worse.
So feeding your dog from your plate is a bad thing then?
Well, not necessarily, as these recipes are specially
designed to be healthy for you and for the dog, so you
can share a meal together every now and then.

Just one word of warning here – always eat your meal
before you give the dog his portion, otherwise he'll
start to think he's the top dog and that will lead to
behavioural problems.

denis' haddock & coriander fish cakes with rice

Imust admit to having a real soft spot for fish cakes, and one of the nurses at the surgery has a dog called Denis who feels the same. I cook up a dish of these in the evening, and then take a leftover cake and a bit of rice into the surgery for Denis the next day. The first time I tried this recipe, I included a bit of Thai curry paste, which I loved – but Denis didn't agree. Since then I've left this out, and we're both very happy with the recipe!

YOU'LL NEED (to make enough for 4 – including the dog!)

- 1kg potatoes
- 400g haddock fillet
- 300ml milk
- 4 tablespoons coriander, chopped
- 4 tablespoons plain flour
- 1 egg, beaten
- 75g breadcrumbs
- 2 tablespoons oil

1. Boil the potatoes for about 15 minutes, until they are nice and soft. Meanwhile put the fish in a large saucepan and cover with the milk. Bring to the boil and then immediately turn off the heat and allow to cook in the juices for five minutes, by which time it should be nice and flaky. Remove from the milk and discard the skin and bones.

2. Mash the potatoes and add in the coriander and the flaked fish. Mix well and form into 8 cakes. Dip each cake in the beaten egg and coat with breadcrumbs. Heat the oil in a frying pan and cook the cakes for about 5 minutes, turning halfway through. Drain with kitchen paper to absorb the oil and serve on a bed of rice.

Did you know ...

that cooking bones makes them prone to splinter? Stick to big raw bones if your dog like a gnaw!

creamy pasta
with chicken & spinach

A quick and easy recipe guaranteed to have you and the dog salivating with anticipation. It's really healthy (for you too) so you can feed this as often as you want – and it's ideal for older dogs as well.

YOU'LL NEED (to make enough for you and the dog)

- 250g pasta
  (any shape will do)
- 1 teaspoon olive oil
- 100g cooked chicken breast
- 1 clove garlic, crushed
- 150ml fromage frais
- 100g spinach, shredded
- 50g parmesan cheese, flaked

1   Cook the pasta in a large pan of boiling water until just tender. Drain and return to the pan.

2   Meanwhile, beak the chicken into small pieces and gently fry with the garlic in the oil for five minutes until crispy and brown. Add in the shredded spinach and continue cooking for a couple of minutes until it has reduced down. Then pour in the fromage frais and cook until the sauce is hot through.

3 Pour the chicken sauce over the pasta, add half the parmesan and toss to mix thoroughly. Sprinkle on the remaining parmesan and serve – hot for you, and cold for the dog.

NUTRITION TIP

If you're trying to get your dog to lose weight, aim to get his weight down by 1–2% per week. So if your dog weighs in at 30kg, he can safely lose 300-600g a week until he's the right weight.

meals to share

sausage & lentil casserole

A great dish for you and the dog to share on a cold winter's evening after a long walk. Lentils are not a bad food for dogs, but they are not totally nutritionally balanced (and can cause wind!) so this is a dish best fed occasionally rather than every day. Reserve it for a particularly wet and cold evening when you both need cheering up with something warm and tasty.

YOU'LL NEED (to make enough for you, the dog and friends)

- 6 sausages
- 1 teaspoon olive oil
- 1 small leek, finely chopped
- 2 garlic cloves, crushed
- 150g Puy lentils
- 600ml chicken stock
- 1 teaspoon balsamic vinegar
- 3 tablespoons parsley, chopped
- Salt and pepper

1 Fry the sausages in the olive oil for 7 or 8 minutes until browned all the way around. Then add in the chopped leek and garlic and cook for a further 5 minutes.

2 Next, add in the lentils and hot stock. Bring to the boil and simmer gently for 45 minutes, until the lentils are tender and most of the stock has been absorbed.

3   Finally, add in the vinegar and parsley, and season with salt and pepper to taste

4   Eat yours while it's still piping hot, but make the dog wait until it has cooled down before spooning out a couple of sausages and sauce into his bowl.

Did you know ...

that dogs with a condition called hypothyroidism have a poor appetite but still put on weight? Luckily it's an easy disease to treat.

meals to share

 shepherd's pie

This delicious recipe has it all – taste, texture and all the nutrients you and the dog need to keep you going. The lamb is ideal, and probably the healthier option, but you can use beef mince if you have some.

The recipe makes one big pie to feed a family and a dog or two.

YOU'LL NEED

- 450g minced lamb (or beef)
- 450g potatoes
- 250ml stock
- 1 leek
- 1 teaspoon olive oil
- 1 carrot
- 50g cheddar cheese
- Cornflour
- Salt and pepper

1 Boil up the spuds and mash, adding a little butter and milk if you like.

2 Chop up the leek and carrot into small pieces and fry gently for five minutes in a little olive oil. Add in the mince and cook for five minutes, stirring frequently, until the meat is browned.

3   Pour in the stock (use a stock cube if you don't have any home made stock), and simmer gently for a couple of minutes. Then mix a little cornflour into a paste with a few drops of water, and stir in to thicken the stock, cooking for a few more minutes.

4   Then, pour the mixture into an ovenproof dish and top with the mashed potato, finishing off with the grated cheese. Cook at (180°C/350°F/Gas 4) for 30–40 minutes.

5   Serve out into dishes, and top your dog's with a sprinkling of his favourite dried kibbles pressed into the potato topping. This adds a bit of crunch and will help to keep his teeth nice and clean. You can skip the dog biscuits in your portion and just brush your teeth!

🐾 taco heaven

'You can't teach an old dog new tricks' or 'El loro viejo no aprende a hablar' as they would say in Mexico. But whoever came up with that saying obviously hadn't tried offering these meaty tacos to the old dog in question, because, believe me, with these on offer even the oldest dog in town will learn something new to get his paws on one!

This taco recipe uses shredded chicken breast, which is very healthy, and I've left out any chillies because dogs are not great fans of spicy foods. The tacos themselves are great for dogs because they are pretty healthy, and lovely and crunchy, and all dogs love a good crunch!

YOU'LL NEED (to make enough filling for 4 tacos – that's three for you and one for the dog)

- 2 medium chicken breasts
- 1 tablespoon olive oil
- 4 cloves garlic
- 1 leek, chopped
- 1 tin refried beans
- 2 teaspoons oregano
- 100g fromage frais

1. Cover the chicken breasts with water and bring to the boil in a medium sized pan. Simmer for about 20 minutes and then remove the chicken but keep hold of the liquid as you'll need this later on. Once the chicken is cool enough to handle, shred it up with your fingers and put on one side.

2. Next, heat the oil in a large saucepan and cook the leek and crushed garlic for five minutes. Add in the tin of refried beans and oregano, and just enough of the broth from the chicken to cover the ingredients. Simmer for 20–25 minutes, until nearly all of the liquid has gone.

3. Fill each taco with the chicken mixture and top with a dollop of fromage frais. Eat yours but make the dog wait for his to cool down.

Did you know ...

that many dog foods only contain 4% meat? Just take a closer look at the ingredients next time you're shopping for pet food.

meals to share

81

 veggie fajitas

You don't have to be a committed veggie to love this, and even Jack, one of the greatest meat eating dogs I've ever known, loves this recipe. So if you feel like a break from meat for a day, and the dog's looking a bit tired of his usual dinner, try out this recipe for a healthy change.

YOU'LL NEED (to feed you, the dog and a friend or two)

- 8 soft flour tortillas
- 2 teaspoons olive oil
- 2 cloves garlic
- 1 green pepper
- 1 red pepper
- 1 small leek
- 1 tin red kidney beans
- ½ teaspoon cumin powder
- 1 teaspoon oregano
- ½ teaspoon paprika

1 Fry the sliced peppers and leek together with the oil, crushed garlic and herbs for 5–7 minutes. Then add in the tin of beans and simmer gently for about ten minutes, until the peppers are tender. Fill up your tortillas with a spoonful of the bean mixture, some shredded lettuce and grated cheese.

2 For the dog, let the mixture cool and then fill his tortillas with a spoonful of mixture and a sprinkling of his normal dog kibbles, just to give a bit of extra crunch.

Goat's milk can make an excellent substitute for bitch's milk for orphaned puppies, especially when egg yolk and a little oil is added. It's more easily digested than cow's milk and is available raw and un-pasteurised.

 # jenny's egg surprise

My wife Jenny has always been a great cook but – being vegetarian – never thought her recipes would appeal to our pets – that is until she caught Jack polishing off the remains of this egg and potato dish we'd had the night before. Now this is one of his (and our) firm favourites, and Jenny always cooks enough for three!

YOU'LL NEED

- 500g potatoes
- 2 large leeks
- 5 eggs
- 120g cheese (Red Leicester is Jack's favourite!)

- 450ml milk
- 40g plain flour
- 40g butter
- 1 teaspoon wholegrain mustard

1 Chop up the potatoes and leeks and boil for twenty minutes or so, until tender, then drain off the water and mash all together. At the same time, hardboil the eggs (8–10 minutes), remove the shells (which you could save to make calcium powder for other recipes) and cut in half.

meals to share

2 Make a cheese sauce by melting the butter in a saucepan over a low heat and stirring in the flour. Cook gently for 2–3 minutes and then add the mustard and remove from the heat. Now gradually add the milk, stirring constantly to avoid lumps. Return to the heat and bring to the boil, still stirring, and simmer for five minutes, stirring occasionally. When smooth and creamy, stir in the cheese a little at a time until melted.

3 Arrange the mashed potatoes and leeks around the edge of a large oven dish and fill the centre with the eggs. Then pour over the cheese sauce and cook in a moderate oven for half an hour.

4 Make sure you wait a good hour before serving to the dog, as it will be piping hot in the middle. Add in some kibbles if you want to clean his teeth as he eats.

spaghetti bolognese

I've got a friend with a dog who refuses to eat anything but this spag bol on a Friday – don't ask me how she knows, but her owner has tried lots of other things to no avail. If there's not a pile of spaghetti in her dish in the evening, she'll sulk off and ignore the family for the rest of the night. So, be warned, this is an addictive recipe, and once your dog has tasted it, it could become a weekly ritual!

YOU'LL NEED (to make a big pan full that'll feed the whole family, dog included)

- 3 rashers bacon, chopped
- 1 leek, finely chopped
- 2 cloves of garlic
- 500g beef, minced
- 1 carrot, diced
- 1 tin tomatoes
- 1 bay leaf
- 1 teaspoon oregano
- 1 teaspoon thyme
- 1 teaspoon balsamic vinegar
- 6-8 sun-dried tomato halves, finely chopped
- Fresh basil leaves
- 500g spaghetti
- 1 teaspoon olive oil
- Lots of fresh grated parmesan cheese

If you and your dog do develop a real taste for this recipe, don't worry – it's very healthy. For the dog's sake I use leek instead of onion (which can damage their red blood cells) and add in some diced veg which is good for you as well. There's also tomato puree, as too much tomato can also be dangerous to dogs.

1   Fry the bacon pieces until starting to go crispy (you shouldn't need to add any oil), then add in the leek and crushed garlic and continue to cook for a few minutes. Add the mince and stir well, breaking up any lumps of meat with a wooden spatula. Cook well until all the meat is brown, and then add the diced carrot and cook for another five minutes, stirring well.

2   Next, add in the tinned tomatoes, bay leaf, herbs, vinegar and finely chopped sun-dried tomatoes. Simmer gently over a low heat for 45 minutes.

3   Cook the spaghetti according to the instructions on the packet, and then toss in a little olive oil before serving.

4   Dish up for the family, and let the dog wait until you've all finished and the bolognese is cool.

Thai chicken fried rice

Not a recipe for every dog out there, but some love it, and it's one of the healthiest recipes I know. There's nothing bad in this at all – just rice, chicken, some crisp veg and a few herbs and spices – so it's suitable for all dogs, even those who are elderly or ill.

If you prefer your food a bit spicy, divide up the ingredients and add a chilli or two to your half, but not to the dog's – they don't usually appreciate hot foods like we do.

YOU'LL NEED (to make enough for two plus the dog)

- 50ml peanut oil (olive oil will do as an alternative)
- 1 small leek, finely chopped
- 2 cloves garlic
- 1 tablespoon brown sugar
- 500g chicken breast fillets, sliced into small strips
- 2 red peppers, sliced thinly
- 200g green beans, chopped in half
- 250g rice
- 2 tablespoons fish sauce
- 2 tablespoons soy sauce
- Handful fresh basil leaves

1 Firstly, cook the rice according to the instructions on the packet and leave to stand.

2 Next, heat the oil in a large wok or frying pan and stir fry the leek and crushed garlic for a few minutes. Add the sugar, stirring until it has dissolved, and then mix in the sliced chicken and stir fry until lightly browned. Mix in the peppers and beans and continue to stir fry until the veg are just tender.

3 Now add the rice and sauces to the wok and stir fry, tossing gently to mix everything together. Remove from the heat after a minute or so and divide into a portion for the dog and the rest for you. Add the basil to yours (and lightly fried chillies if you like) but leave the dog's portion plain.

Did you know ...

that some protein is better than others? The best protein for your dog comes from meat, so avoid pet foods which have soya or vegetable protein.

meals to share

meals for older dogs

When you're looking after an elderly dog, it's even more important to get their diet spot on, than when they were younger. Older animals can't tolerate high levels of proteins or fats and need to eat a diet that meets their specific nutritional needs. They generally need less energy, and a bit more fibre, and although they need a reasonable amount of protein to keep them in shape, too much will put a strain on their kidneys. Ideally you should feed a diet based on proteins like chicken and fish that can be used most efficiently, and avoid foods with beef and other red meat proteins.

The best way of making sure your older dog is getting just the right mix of nutrients he needs is to feed him a top quality dried complete food. Choose one without artificial additives like preservatives and flavourings, and aim for a protein level of around 18–22% (adult dog foods usually have about 22–26% protein).

However, just because your dog is getting on a bit, doesn't mean you have to stop cooking him the occasional home-cooked meal – far from it. Giving him a healthy treat with one of these recipes is a great way of topping up his reservoirs of vitamins and nutrients, and they're all specially formulated so as not to put a strain on the kidneys. They've also got some stronger flavours, as older dogs don't smell as well as they used to (in more ways than one in some cases ...).

Just like humans, dogs need vitamin E to keep nasty 'free-radicals' at bay. These molecules contribute to ageing and lots of degenerative diseases, so making sure your dog's diet has plenty of vitamin E is vital. It is found in many green plants and vegetables.

chicken, spinach & fish mash

Now our dog Jack might not be exactly what you'd call elderly at the moment, but when I was trying out this recipe he absolutely loved it. The combination of the easy-to-digest protein from the chicken, with the good quality carbohydrate from the sweet potato, and the vitamins from the spinach make it super healthy – and the sardines add in essential omega-3 oils as well as a bit of extra taste.

YOU'LL NEED

- 250g chicken mince
- 400g sweet potatoes
- 250g spinach, shredded
- 1 tin sardines in oil
- ½ teaspoon egg shell powder (see Fishy Delight) or 1x1000mg calcium supplement, crushed.
- 1 teaspoon brewer's yeast

1 Boil the sweet potatoes in their skins until tender (about ten minutes) and then drain and mash them. At the same time, gently fry the chicken mince, until it is cooked through, then add the spinach and cook for a few minutes until reduced.

2 Finally, add the sardines, along with all the oil, to the mince and spinach, and mix it all together with the mash in a mixing bowl. Add in the calcium or egg shell, and the brewer's yeast and form into egg-sized balls.

meals for older dogs

old dog power juice

There's no doubt that fresh fruit and veg help to keep old age at bay – lots of studies have proved that eating plenty of fruit and veg reduces the risk of all sorts of diseases, including cancer. Getting a dog, especially an old boy, to eat down a plate of fruit and veg is nigh on impossible – which is why I've come up with this cunning recipe for a revitalising juice drink which old dogs will love. Feed this once a week and you'll keep him fighting fit for years to come!

YOU'LL NEED

- 300g assorted fruit and veg – anything you have to hand (except onions, tomatoes and mushrooms)

- 100g chicken liver

1 Put the liver in a small bowl and pour over just enough boiling water to cover. Let it stand for ten minutes.

2 Meanwhile, chuck all the veg and fruit into the blender. Anything goes here – apples, plums, cabbage, courgettes, carrots – as long as it's fruit or veg and it's not an onion, tomato or mushroom, in it goes. Whiz it all up to make a thick puree. Then add in the liver, complete with its water.

3 Blend together, adding more water if necessary, until you have a thick drink. Pour a reasonable amount into the dog bowl and watch her slurp it up. You can freeze the rest if you have some left over.

NUTRITION TIP

Want to know if your dog is overweight? – it's easy to check by feeling his ribs. Run a hand over his chest and if you can easily feel his ribs, he's OK. If all you can feel is soft fatty tissue and you're struggling to find his ribs underneath, the chances are he's overweight.

 spanish omelette

Eggs are sometimes referred to as 'the perfect protein source' because they contain such a well balanced mix of amino acids, making them easy to digest and use. This is very important for older dogs, as any waste left behind in the body from eating less good proteins (such as beef) can damage the kidneys.

This simple omelette recipe uses a beef stock cube to add a bit of meaty taste, and potato and carrot for carbohydrate and vitamins. A normal Spanish Omelette would contain onions, but I've left them out as they can be harmful, especially for older dogs.

It's ideal as an occasional treat, just to put a bit of bounce back into those old legs.

YOU'LL NEED (for a two-dog omelette)

- 4 eggs
- A little milk
- 1 stock cube
- Olive oil
- 1 potato
- 1 carrot

1. Dice the carrot and potato and boil them for about 7–8 minutes – until they are just about edible but not too soft. Then heat up a little olive oil in a good non-stick frying pan and gently fry the veg until it is browned and tender.

2. Meanwhile beat the eggs with a little milk and the stock cube in a large mixing bowl. When the veg is done, pour into the egg mixture and mix together. Then add a little more oil to the pan and heat until it is just smoking, pour in the egg and veg mixture.

3. Cook for about five minutes, shaking gently from side to side to keep it from sticking, and then turn over, using a plate. Do the other side with a little more oil and then turn out onto a plate and allow to cool. Serve with an 'olé' and a glass of Rioja (for yourself of course!).

NUTRITION TIP

Some dogs hate the taste of tap water as it has chlorine in – so if your dog turns his nose up at his water bowl, try offering him rainwater from a water butt, or even bottled water if you're feeling very generous!

meals for older dogs

white fish & rice

Dog food doesn't get much healthier than this, and the added coriander will help tickle the older dog's taste buds. It's got a moderate level of protein, which is all highly digestible, meaning less work for the kidneys.

YOU'LL NEED (to feed a couple of hungry hounds)

- 250g white fish fillet
- 300ml milk
- 1 teaspoon fresh lemon juice
- 1 teaspoon olive oil
- 1 tablespoon fresh coriander
- 125g brown rice

1 Put the rice on to cook as brown rice takes a good half an hour. Then cover the fish with the milk, bring to the boil and then remove from the heat, allowing the fish to cook in hot milk for about 5 minutes.

2 Then remove the fish from the milk and crumble it into a dish with the lemon juice and oil. Mix in the cooked and drained rice and finally add the chopped up coriander.

special meals

There are times in your dog's life when he might need some special attention to his diet – perhaps he's under the weather and needs a healthy boost, or maybe he's just got a bit too big around the middle and would benefit from some low-calorie treats to help get him back into shape.

These recipes are specially designed to address particular problems, so if your dog isn't quite right, have a look through this section and see if there's a recipe that fits the bill.

🐾 chicken soup
– for the sickly dog

This recipe is full of goodness from the chicken and veg, and it's easily eaten and digested. If your dog is a bit below par, or recovering from something more serious, this recipe is ideal and guaranteed to get him back on the road to recovery.

YOU'LL NEED

- 2 chicken drumsticks
- 1 carrot
- 1 potato
- 1 teaspoon parsley
- 1 stock cube

It's really easy this one – just cover the chicken and chopped up veg with boiling water and simmer on a low heat for thirty minutes. Then fish out the chicken, remove the bones and return the meat to the pan. Sprinkle in the parsley and allow to cool. Best served slightly warm, with Joe & Jack's natural dried food sprinkled in as croutons!

special meals

 low-fat treats

If the dog is looking a little tubby around the middle, but he lives for his daily treat (or two), here's a recipe for some biscuits that will keep him satisfied, but won't pile on quite so many pounds.

YOU'LL NEED (for a couple of average portions)

- ½ pint (250ml) hot water
- 1 beef stock cube
- 2 tablespoons olive oil
- 4 cups whole wheat flour
- 1 stick celery, finely chopped
- 1 carrot, grated

1   Dissolve the stock cube in the hot water and add to the flour and vegetables in a large mixing bowl. Add the stock gradually to form a thick dough, which you can roll out on a well-floured surface to 1 cm thick. Then cut out small biscuit shapes using a knife or the end of an apple corer. Try to make the biscuits a little bit smaller than normal – every little helps when it comes to cutting down the calories!

2   Place the biscuits on a greased baking tray and cook in a moderate over for about half an hour. Allow to cool and ration with steely determination! (Store in the fridge in an airtight container for several weeks.)

special meals

🐾 yoghurt chicken & rice – for the dog with diarrhoea

There are lots of possible causes of diarrhoea, ranging from nasty infections to dietary insensitivities, but the treatment often has one thing in common – a period of starvation (often 24 hours) followed by the use of a really bland diet for a few days. This regime is often sufficient to sort out most mild cases of diarrhoea, and it's a sensible first step to consider rather than rushing to the vet straight away (obviously if this doesn't do the trick, or the dog is really unwell, you should get him straight to the surgery for a proper check over).

This recipe is particularly good because both chicken and rice are very easily digested and unlikely to irritate the bowel, and the live yoghurt provides probiotics which help to restore the correct balance of good bacteria in the gut.

YOU'LL NEED (for a couple of average portions)

- **200g chicken mince**
- **½ cup of rice** (preferably brown)
- **Plain, live yoghurt**

1. Add the rice and the mince to a large pan of boiling water. Cooking them together in this way means the flavour of the meat soaks deep into the rice, making it much more palatable (which is important for such a bland meal).

2. When the rice is cooked, drain away the water and allow the mixture to cool.

For each serving, mix with a tablespoon of yoghurt (for a Labrador-sized dog).

NUTRITION TIP

Small dogs are fully grown at 9–12 months of age, but some big breeds such as Great Danes are still growing until they are 2 years old!

special meals

🐾 beefy rice
– for the diabetic dog

If your dog has been diagnosed with diabetes, you'll be aware of the importance of getting her diet just right. Diabetes is a disease of the sugar control system in the body, and is generally treated in dogs by using injections of insulin, which reduce the level of sugar in the blood. These injections are only half the story though, as diet is just as crucial in keeping a good control of the amount of sugar in the system.

The ideal diet for a diabetic dog will contain lots of so-called 'complex carbohydrates' such as starch, and also plenty of fibre, while having low levels of simple sugars. This reduces the peaks and troughs of sugar in the blood by releasing energy gradually through the day.

The best way of getting this kind of diet right is to feed a specially formulated commercial diet from your vet. But that doesn't mean you can't treat her to the occasional home-cooked meal. As long as you stick to recipes like this one, which are low in sugar and high in starch and fibre, you can definitely cook up something tasty once a week or so, just to add a little variety to her life.

This basic diabetes recipe provides approximately 50% complex carbohydrates, which is ideal.

YOU'LL NEED

- 750ml water
- 1 stock cube
- 450g lean beef, cubed
- 1 carrot, grated
- 1 stick of celery, finely chopped
- 100g broccoli, finely chopped
- 100g spinach
- 150g brown rice

1   Boil up the water and dissolve the stock cube in it. Then drop in the beef and simmer for about twenty minutes. Fish out the beef once cooked and set aside in a large bowl with the grated and finely chopped veg. Put the rice into the boiling stock and cook for about 30 minutes until tender (less if you are using white rice).

2   Then drain any remaining water off the rice and pour the rice over the veg and meat, mixing well. The hot, moist rice will effectively steam the grated veggies, so they can be easily digested, but don't lose any nutrients.

3   Allow this mixture to cool and then feed. It can be frozen in single serving bags, so you can defrost one every week or so.

special meals

venison/rabbit/duck & potato – the hypoallergenic diet

Food intolerances and allergies are relatively common in dogs and can be problematic. Intolerances are where the dog can't digest a certain food, such as milk, whereas allergies are more serious and involve nasty reactions to food including itching skin and diarrhoea.

If your dog has a food intolerance or allergy, your vet will probably recommend a suitable hypoallergenic diet which is free of the particular foods your dog reacts to. Whilst it is ideal to stick to this food as much as you can, there is nothing wrong with cooking a tasty meal for you dog every now and then as long as it is also free of whatever is causing your dog's symptoms.

This recipe is designed to suit most intolerant or allergic dogs, but it's important to check with your vet before using this, or any recipe, to make sure it won't cause problems.

YOU'LL NEED (for several meals – it is easily freezable)

- 450g venison, rabbit or duck – minced*
- 450g potatoes
- 2 eggs
- 2 carrots

* Most dogs will be fine on venison, rabbit or duck, but obviously avoid any of these if your vet advises that your dog could be allergic or intolerant to them.

1   Dice the potatoes and carrots, boil them until tender and then drain and mash together. Meanwhile, hardboil the eggs and, when done (8 minutes), crush up one of the shells and add the fine powder, plus both eggs, to the potato mash.

2   Fry the minced meat until cooked through, using a little olive oil if necessary, and then add to the mash and mix in thoroughly.

Did you know ...

that chocolate can kill your dog? It contains a chemical called theobromine which can cause serious illness and even death in some dogs, so make sure you keep your chocolate stash just for you!

special meals

balanced chicken & rice – for dogs with kidney or liver disease

As dogs get older, many will suffer from liver and/or kidney disease, with symptoms ranging from weight loss to vomiting and collapse. Treating these two problems can be very tricky, and diet is an essential part of helping your dog cope. Once your dog has been diagnosed as suffering from liver or kidney disease, your vet may well recommend a special prescription diet for him, which contains the ideal levels of nutrients he needs to limit the deterioration of the condition.

However, just because he's on this special diet, it doesn't necessarily mean that home cooking is out of the window. It is possible to cook the occasional special meal for your dog, as long as you stick to a recipe which meets the following requirements:

- Slightly reduced protein level
- Good quality protein – fish and chicken are ideal
- Low phosphorus – so avoid dairy foods and rich deep green veg like spinach
- High moisture content

This recipe provides a tasty alternative to the prescription foods for liver and kidney disease, and is ideal as a once-a-week treat:

YOU'LL NEED (for several meals – it is easily freezable)

- 100g brown rice
- 200g chicken mince
- 1 carrot, grated
- 1 teaspoon calcium carbonate (from your health food shop)
- 1 multivitamin tablet

1   Simply boil up the rice until almost cooked (about 25 minutes) and then drop in the grated carrot and continue to simmer until the rice is tender. Meanwhile, brown the mince in a frying pan (without oil) until cooked through.

2   When the rice is cooked, drain away the water and add in the mince. Crush up the multivitamin and add with the calcium to the mix.

special meals

The Joe & Jack's story

Home cooking for your dog is a great way of giving him high-quality food packed full of natural nutrients – but it's not the only way. With the experience I've gained from creating these recipes, and the help of Pets' Kitchen, a new natural pet food company, I've developed my own range of healthy complete foods for dogs.

All my new foods, which are called Joe & Jack's after my dog Jack who's been the chief taste-tester, are made using the same real, natural ingredients as I use in my home-cooking, including fresh chicken and lamb, and have absolutely no artificial additives at all. In fact, I'm so confident about the quality of the ingredients that I even did a 100-mile charity walk eating nothing but Joe & Jack's!

My main aim with Joe & Jack's has been to offer dog owners the chance to feed their pets foods which are as good as the food they eat themselves. Diet is just as crucial for our dogs as it is for us, and by using the same ingredients and principles as found in foods for humans, I've created a range of foods that offer our canine friends the very best in fresh, healthy nutrition.

The recipes for Joe & Jack's combine my own veterinary knowledge with that of the pet nutritionists at Pets' Kitchen – and the input of Jack and many of my canine patients from the surgery!

For more information, visit the Joe & Jack's website at www.joeandjacks.co.uk.

The author

Since starring in the BBC1 hit series 'Vets in Practice', Joe Inglis has managed to juggle the demands of being a vet with a blossoming and diverse media career. This has included presenting roles in many television programmes, most notably Blue Peter, as well as writing books, and contributing to magazines and newspapers.

Joe qualified as a veterinary surgeon from Bristol University in 1996 and he is recognised as a leading authority in pet nutrition. He attributes his passion for the natural world and great spirit of adventure to being a direct descendent of Charles Darwin (his great-great-great-grandson to be precise!).

Other Joe Inglis books & DVDs

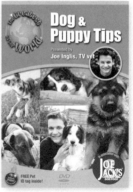

all available from **www.**the**greatest**inthe**world**.com